Contributing Editor
Andrea Tropeano, M.A.

Cover Artist
Brenda DiAntonis

Editor in Chief
Ina Massler Levin, M.A.

Creative Director
Karen J. Goldfluss, M.S. Ed.

Art Production Manager
Kevin Barnes

Art Coordinator
Renée Christine Yates

Imaging
Rosa C. See

Publisher

Mary D. Smith, M.S. Ed.

CELEBRATE THE HOLIDAYS!

Grades 1-3

For each holiday you will find:

- A Little Book
- Cross-Curricular Activities
- Historical Facts
- Holiday Journals

Chinese New Year. This celebration lasts 15 days. Parades are a big part of the new year. L...

Cinco de Mayo

Teacher Created Resources, Inc.
6421 Industry Way
Westminster, CA 92683
www.teachercreated.com

ISBN: 978-1-4206-2058-0

© 2008 Teacher Created Resources, Inc.
Made in U.S.A.

Teacher Created Resources

Table of Contents

Introduction

Celebrating holidays can be wonderful opportunities for children to learn about the traditions and values that are cherished parts of people's lives. Learning about other cultures and their traditions is also a significant part of education. Unfortunately, in today's world, teachers struggle with how to fit everything into their daily schedule. Teachers have little time to incorporate holiday celebrations into their busy day. This book provides teachers with cross curricular holiday activities that are quick, easy, and do not require many outside materials. The activities chosen present each holiday in an educational manner while at the same time they engage students' interest with a fun activity.

Each holiday section contains historical facts, suggestions for activities, a reproducible mini book, a cross curricular activity, and a journaling page. Each holiday is introduced with a list of historical facts followed by suggestions for fun activities that can be done at the desire of the teacher. A literacy component is included in the form of a mini book. A cross curricular activity such as an art, craft, game, or puzzle is incorporated into each holiday. These activities are easy for the busy teacher to prepare and incorporate into their curriculum. Finally, each holiday includes a journaling page that can be used as a culminating writing activity. The teacher may wish to use the journaling page as an assessment tool to see how much each student has learned about the presented holiday.

Instructions for Mini Books

1. Reproduce minibook page for each student*
2. Color illustrations.
3. Cut pages on dashed lines.
4. Arrange pages in numerical order.
5. Place cover page on top.
6. Secure at the top using either a staple or a paper fastener.

   * Teachers may wish to enlarge minibook for younger children.

Meeting Standards

Listed below are the McREL standards and benchmarks for Language Arts Level 1 (Grades K–2), which are used with permission from McREL (Copyright 2007, McREL, Mid-continent Research for Education and Learning. Telephone: 303/337-0990. Website: www.mcrel.org .)

McREL standards are in bold and benchmarks are in regular print.

Uses the stylistic and rhetorical aspects of writing

- Uses descriptive words to convey basic ideas
- Uses declarative and interrogative sentences in written composition

Uses grammatical and mechanical conventions in written composition

- Uses conventions of print in writing (e.g., forms letters in print, uses upper-and-lowercase letters of the alphabet, spaces words and sentences, writes from left-to-right and top-to-bottom, includes margins
- Uses complete sentences in written compositions
- Uses nouns in written compositions (e.g., nouns for simple objects, family members, community workers, and categories)
- Uses verbs in written compositions (e.g., verbs for a variety of situations, action words)
- Uses adjectives in written compositions (e.g., uses descriptive words)
- Uses adverbs in written compositions (e.g., uses words that answer how, when, where, and why questions)

New Year's Day Fun

New Year's Day Facts

- Celebrating the New Year on January 1 began over 2000 years ago in Rome, Italy.

- People celebrate the new year in different ways all over the world.

- In the United States, some people celebrate by eating black-eyed peas and greens.

- Some people believe eating certain food will bring prosperity in the new year.

- Making New Year's resolutions is another tradition. A resolution is the decision to make a change for the better.

- Father Time represents the old year and a baby in diapers represents the New Year.

- Other countries celebrate by meditation, family gatherings, fishing, and parties.

- In the United States, New Year's Eve is celebrated at midnight.

New Year's Day Fun Activities

1. Make New Year's resolutions.

2. Find out what foods are special in your area and prepare them for a festive meal.

3. Have a class New Year's Day party and have a "pretend" countdown to the new year.

4. Group beans, buttons, pennies, etc., into sets of 100 to represent the number for the coming year.

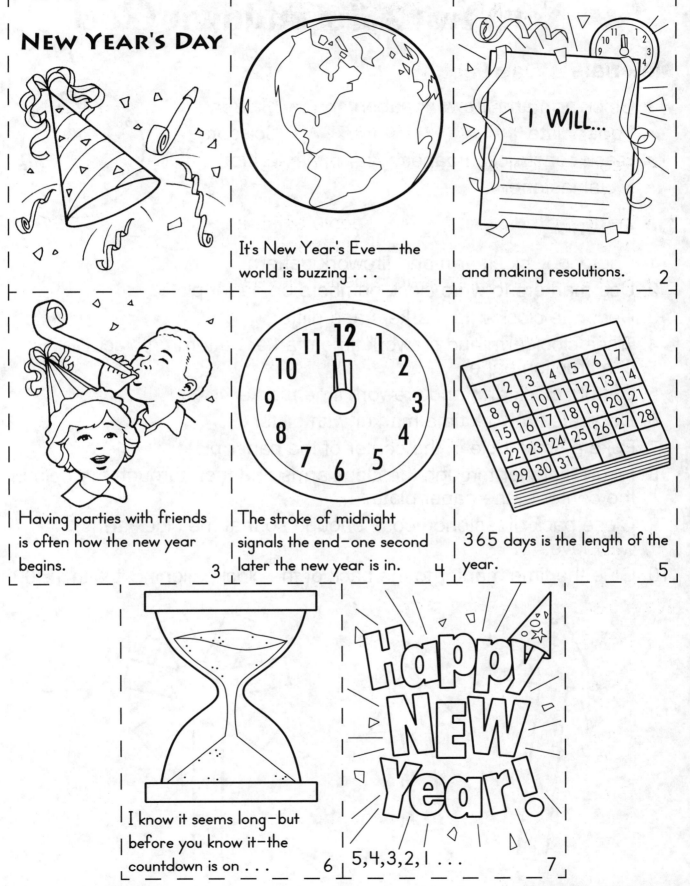

NEW YEAR'S DAY

It's New Year's Eve—the world is buzzing . . .

I WILL...

and making resolutions. 2

Having parties with friends is often how the new year begins. 3

The stroke of midnight signals the end—one second later the new year is in. 4

365 days is the length of the year. 5

I know it seems long—but before you know it—the countdown is on . . . 6

Happy NEW Year!

5, 4, 3, 2, 1 . . . 7

New Year's Countdown Clock

Materials

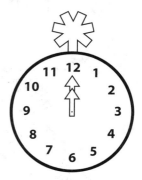

- Clock arm and firework pattern
- Paper plate
- Black construction paper
- Metal fastener
- Markers
- Scissors
- Glitter

Directions

1. Photocopy clock arm and firework pattern.
2. Use markers to write clock numbers on paper plate.
3. Decorate clock with markers and glitter.
4. Trace clock arm and firework time marker pattern on black construction paper.
5. Cut out clock arm and firework time marker.
6. Decorate firework time marker with glitter.
7. Poke a small hole in the center of the paper plate.
8. Insert fastener through the clock arms and then through the hole in the center of the paper plate.
9. Close back of fastener loose enough so that the clock arms will move.
10. Glue the time marker to the back of the clock, aligning it with 12:00.

I Know About New Year's Day

Martin Luther King, Jr. Day Fun

Martin Luther King, Jr. Facts

- Martin Luther King, Jr. was a famous African American leader.

- Martin Luther King, Jr. was born in Atlanta, Georgia, on January 15, 1929. He was the son of a minister.

- He became a civil rights leader. He believed in non-violence, and peaceful solutions to problems.

- Martin Luther King, Jr. is remembered for his famous "I Have A Dream . . ." speech. This speech was given at a civil rights demonstration in Washington, D.C., on August 28, 1963.

- Martin Luther King, Jr. died tragically on April 4, 1968, in Memphis, Tennessee.

- January 15th is a national holiday to remember Dr. Martin Luther King, Jr. It is a day to think of justice, equality, and peace in our world.

Martin Luther King, Jr. Day Fun Activities

1. Role-play how to solve conflicts peacefully.

2. Designate a student to be the class "peace-maker" to help solve conflicts.

3. Create an acrostic poem, using the word "PEACE."

4. Invite a police officer to visit the class and discuss his/her involvement in peacemaking.

5. Read a short biography of Dr. Martin Luther King, Jr. and find out how his birthday became a national holiday.

Martin Luther King, Jr. Day

I have a dream

This is Martin Luther King, Jr. He is a famous African American.

He dreamed of a peaceful world.

2

He shared his dream with many people.

3

"I have a dream . . .", is what he said.

4

Martin Luther King, Jr. died fighting for equality.

5

He is remembered for his dream of equality, justice, and peace.

6

His dream still lives on today.

7

Martin Luther King, Jr. Stamp

Reproduce this page to create a stamp honoring Martin Luther King, Jr. Use the space at the bottom of the stamp to write a few words that represent your picture.

Handshake

Materials

- Pencil
- Cuff pattern
- Construction paper in colors that represent skin tones
- White construction paper
- Scissors
- Glue
- Round head fasteners

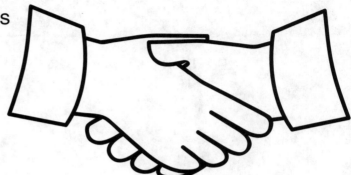

Directions

1. Trace hand on two different shades of skin toned construction paper
2. Cut out both hands
3. Trace cuff pattern on white construction paper
4. Cut out cuffs
5. Glue cuffs to the wrist of both hands
6. Place hands together forming a handshake
7. Use fasteners to attach hands together
8. On the back of hands, have each students write one reason why people shake hands

I Know About
Martin Luther King, Jr. Day

Groundhog Day Fun

Groundhog Day Facts

- Groundhog Day is on February 2nd. On this date people watch the groundhog to help them predict the weather. The most famous groundhog is Punxsutawney Phil.

- There is a legend which states that if the groundhog does not see his shadow when he ends his hibernation, then we will have an early spring. However, if the groundhog does see his shadow when he comes out, then we will have at least six more weeks of winter.

- A groundhog is also known as a woodchuck. Groundhogs live in Canada and the Eastern and Midwestern United States. They are small, brown in color, and are members of the squirrel family.

- Groundhogs make their homes in burrows or dens underground. They hibernate from October to February.

- Groundhogs are plant-eating mammals. Their normal life span is 4 to 5 years.

- Groundhogs are diurnal creatures. They are awake in the daytime.

Groundhog Day Fun Activities

1. Measure shadows, using standard and non-standard measurement tools (e.g., shoe lengths, paper clips, straws).

2. Play "shadow chase." Choose one person in the group to be "it." His or her goal is to step on another player's shadow. When the person who is "it" steps on the shadow of another player, that player becomes "it." Continue the game in this manner.

3. Write a letter to join Punxsutawney Phil's Fan Club:

   Phil's Fan Club
   Punxsutawney Groundhog Club
   Chamber of Commerce
   124 West Mahoning Street
   Punxsutawney, PA 15767

Mr. Groundhog, What Will It Be?

Coats and mittens or shorts and a top?

Will I go sledding or play in the sandbox?

2

Hurry out Mr. Groundhog so I can see how to make plans with my family.

3

See your shadow—run and hide six more weeks I'll be inside.

4

But if you don't see your shadow today—

5

. . . I will be ready to run outside and play!

6

What did Mr. Groundhog predict this year? —6 more weeks of winter or spring is here!

7

Shadow Time

Preparation

Copy the following patterns onto white construction paper for everyone in your class.

Materials

- Two patterns (groundhog and hole)
- Scissors
- Crayon
- Craft stick
- Paste
- Flashlight

Directions

1. Color and cut out both patterns.
2. Paste a craft stick onto the back of the groundhog.
3. Cut a slit for the groundhog to poke through the hole.
4. Use a flashlight to create a shadow for the groundhog.

Shadow Time *(cont.)*

Groundhog Pattern

16

Shadow Time *(cont.)*

Groundhog's Hole Pattern

I Know About Groundhog Day

Chinese New Year Fun

Chinese New Year Facts

- Chinese New Year is celebrated in late January or early February by Chinese people all over the world.

- The festive celebration lasts about 15 days.

- For the Chinese people, red symbolizes happiness. Red is worn during Chinese New Year.

- Parades are a part of the Chinese New Year celebration.

- Lions and lion dancers are also special. It is believed that the lion will scare away evil and bring good luck.

- The dragon is the national symbol of China. In the Chinese tradition, the dragon represents royalty and is a protector.

- Fireworks and firecrackers are a part of the Chinese New Year festivities.

- A Lantern Festival ends the Chinese New Year.

Chinese New Year Fun Activities

1. Find out when Chinese New Year begins this year. Find out what animal is the symbol for the year.

2. Find out what animal is the symbol of your birth year.

3. Locate China on a globe. Discuss how far it is from your country to China.

4. Discuss possible modes of transportation from your country to China.

5. Make a Chinese flag.

6. Have a tasting party. Try fortune cookies, stir-fry vegetables, and egg rolls. Practice using chopsticks.

7. Have a parade around the school or neighborhood wearing dragon hats.

8. Learn the phrase "Gung Hay Fat Choy" which means "Happy New Year."

The Chinese New Year

The Chinese New Year begins in late January or early February.

It lasts for 15 days. It is celebrated by Chinese people all over the world.

2

A lot of time is spent getting ready for the celebration.

3

People have parades.

4

The parade is led by a dragon.

5

There are firecrackers too.

6

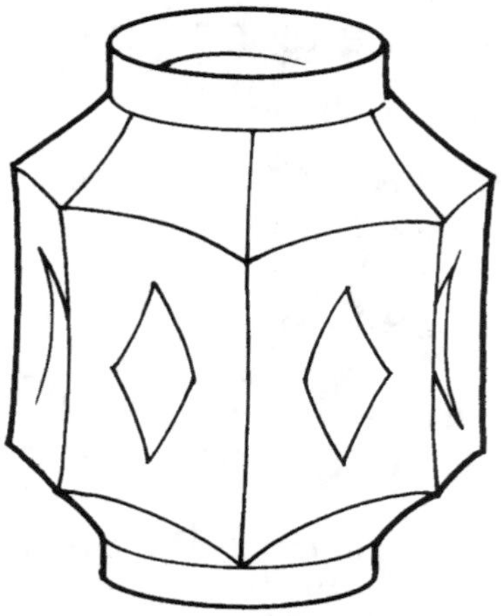

The celebration ends with a Lantern Festival.

7

Paper Lantern

Materials

- Construction paper
- Tape
- Scissors

Directions

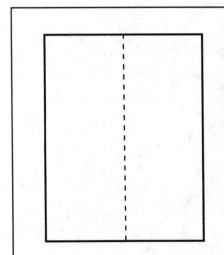

1. Fold construction paper in half lengthwise

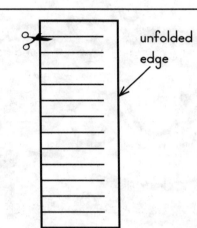

2. Cut paper strips beginning at fold and ending about one inch before unfolded edge of paper

unfolded edge

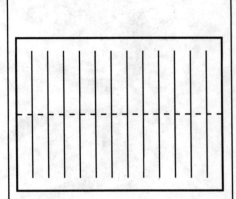

3. Unfold paper horizontally

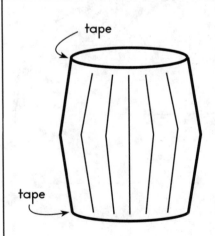

tape

tape

4. Roll the paper so in is shaped like a lantern and tape the two ends together

5. Cut out a strip of different colored paper and tape it to the top of the lantern as a handle

* Optional: Use glitter and Chinese symbols to decorate lantern.

I Know About Chinese New Year

22

Valentine's Day Fun

Valentine's Day Facts

- Valentine's Day is celebrated on February 14th.

- Valentine's Day is a day to express feelings of love to friends and family.

- This holiday began in Rome, Italy, hundreds of years ago.

- It is believed that Valentine's Day got its name from St. Valentine. St. Valentine was a Christian bishop who cared about people, especially children.

- Many people exchange gifts, cards, candy, and flowers on this day.

- On Valentine's Day, many gifts are heart-shaped. Heart-shaped gifts represent love.

- Cupid is a symbol of love. Cupid has a bow and an arrow. It is believed, if someone is "hit" with Cupid's arrow, then he or she will fall in love.

Valentine's Day Fun Activities

1. Sort and graph different-colored heart-shaped candy.

2. Estimate the number of candy hearts in a jar.

3. Put candy hearts in sets of ten and count.

4. List as many red foods as possible.

5. Bake a heart-shaped cake for a Valentine's Day party.

6. Talk about the human heart. Discuss its functions.

Valentine's Day

I love Valentine's Day!

How about you?

2

Cupid, flowers and candy too!

3

February 14th is the day that we celebrate "love" in a special way.

4

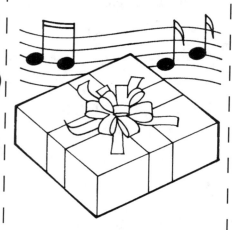

There are poems, songs, and presents too.

5

Will you be my valentine?

6

I LOVE YOU

7

Tissue Paper Heart Card

Materials

- Tissue paper cut into small squares
- Construction paper
- Scissors
- Pencil
- Glue

Directions

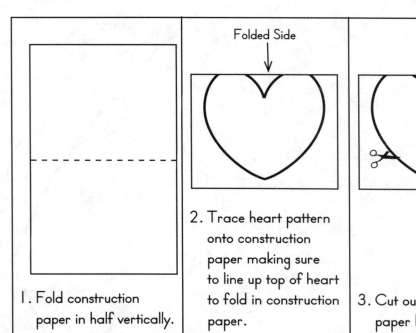
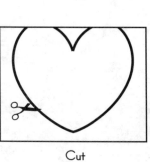
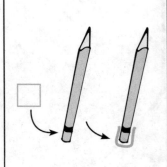

1. Fold construction paper in half vertically.

2. Trace heart pattern onto construction paper making sure to line up top of heart to fold in construction paper.

3. Cut out construction paper heart.

4. Take tissue paper squares and wrap around pencil or finger.

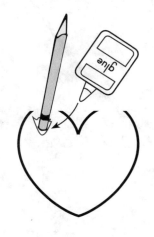

Dear Mom,

5. Glue tissue paper pieces to top of heart card.

6. Write a Valentines Day message on inside the cards.

Heart Pattern

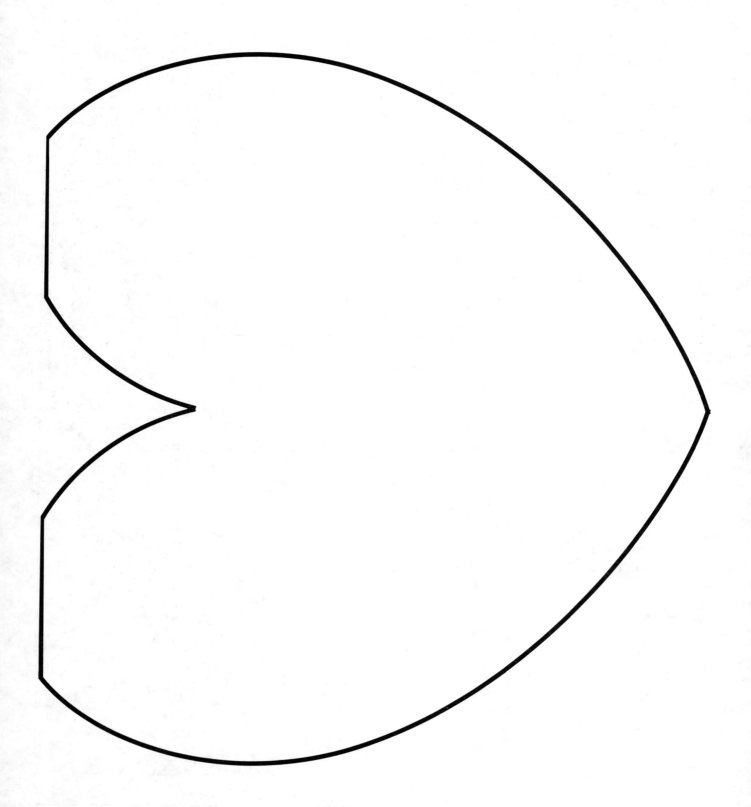

I Know About Valentine's Day

Presidents' Day Fun

Presidents' Day Facts

- Presidents' Day is celebrated on the third Monday in February.

- Two great presidents are remembered on this day—George Washington and Abraham Lincoln.

- George Washington was born on February 22, 1732. He is known as "The Father of Our Country" because he was our first president.

- George Washington was known for his leadership and honesty.

- George Washington's face is on the quarter.

- Abraham Lincoln was born on February 12, 1809, in Kentucky. He was our 16th president.

- Abraham Lincoln lived in a log cabin.

- Abraham Lincoln was the president who freed the slaves.

- Abraham Lincoln's face is on the penny.

Presidents' Day Fun Activities

1. Identify the number of presidents from George Washington to the present.

2. Construct Lincoln's log cabin, using pretzels, craft sticks, or twigs.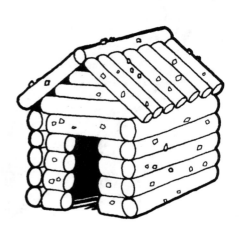

3. Write about what you would do as president.

4. Make and eat a "George Washington" cherry pie.

5. Talk about the symbols of our country.

6. Vote on something important to the class.

Presidents' Day

Presidents are important. They have lots to do –

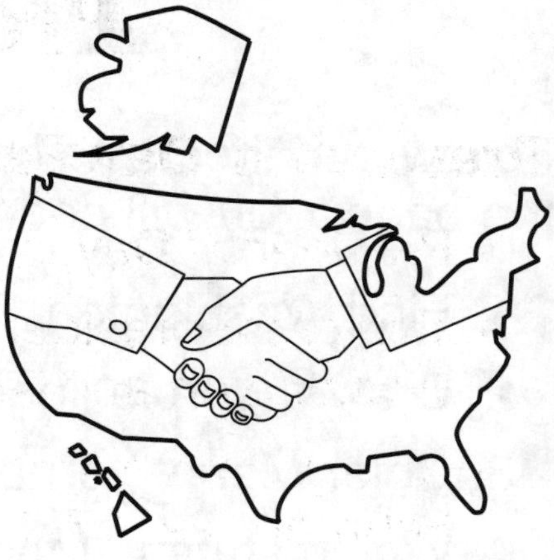

to keep peace in our country

2

and the world too.

3

Washington and Lincoln – quite an important two – they were leaders when our country was new.

4

We live in a great country.

5

Yes, that is true.

6

Presidents' Day is a time to honor presidents, old and new.

7

A "Washington" Map

Follow the directions below. All answers can be found on the map on the page. You will need crayons to complete this page.

1. Find Washington, D.C. On the (•) draw a (★), and color it yellow.
2. Draw a purple line south from Washington, D.C., to Mount Vernon.
3. Color Mount Vernon orange.
4. Which state is Mount Vernon located in ? _____
   Color this state green.
5. Find the Atlantic Ocean. Color it blue.
6. What is the name of the river that is next to Washington, D.C. ?

   _____

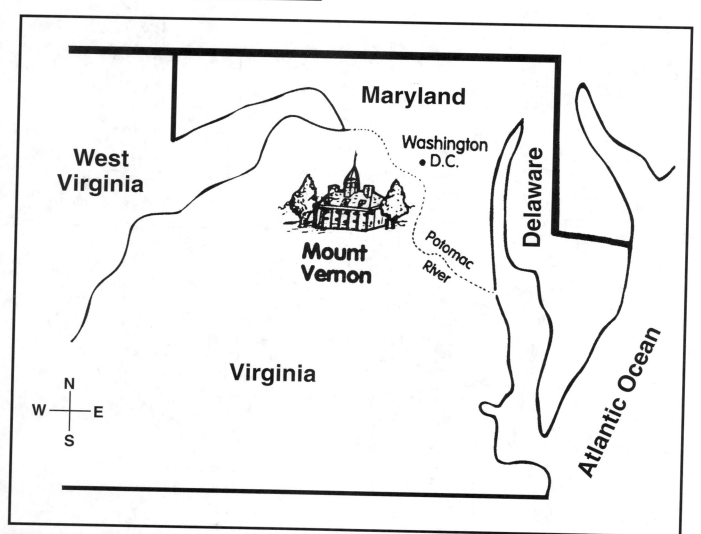

Lincoln's Homes

Abraham Lincoln was born in Kentucky. When he was seven years old, his family moved to Indiana. Fourteen years later they moved to Illinois.

1. Write the answers for each problem in the circle provided.

2. Connect the numbers in the circles in 1-2-3 order to trace Lincoln's route from home to home.

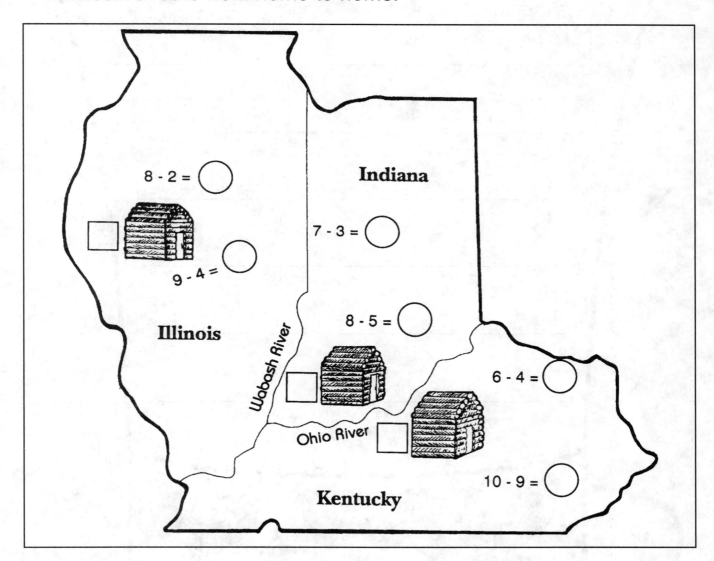

*Write a 1 in the square next to Lincoln's first home.

*Write a 2 in the square next to Lincoln's second home.

*Write a 3 in the square next to Lincoln's third home.

I Know About Presidents' Day

St. Patrick's Day Fun

St. Patrick's Day Facts

- St. Patrick's Day is celebrated on March 17th.

- St. Patrick's Day is a day to think about all of the people who have traveled from different countries to live in America.

- St. Patrick's Day got its name from St. Patrick. St. Patrick taught many Irish people about Christianity and how to read and write.

- Some of the ways St. Patrick's Day is celebrated are wearing green, making and eating green foods, and having parties.

- In the United States, there are special parades on St. Patrick's Day.

- The shamrock is a national emblem of Ireland. Many people decorate with shamrocks.

- Stories of leprechauns are told on this day. The leprechauns of Irish legends are little men who have pots of hidden gold. The legend states that if you find a leprechaun, he must give you all his gold.

St. Patrick's Day Fun Activities

1. Have a "green food" tasting party. Use green gelatin, pickles, green sherbet, salad, green punch, etc.

2. Make shamrock-shaped potato printers. Dip the printers into green paint and press onto paper. Sprinkle with golden glitter and let dry.

3. Locate Ireland on the globe. Determine how far it is from your country to Ireland.

4. Play Irish songs and dance an Irish jig.

5. Wear green.

St. Patrick's Day

St. Patrick was a preacher in a land far away. He helped many people in his own way.

He lived in Ireland—a land of green.

2

March 17 is St. Patrick's Day.

It is celebrated in many ways—

3

stories of leprechauns, luck and wishes

4

and pots of gold to name a few.

5

Wear green on St. Patrick's Day

6

to keep the pinches away!

7

Green Riddles

1. I am a precious gem used to make fine jewelry. I am mined mainly in South America. What am I?

_____

2. I am a tart fruit. I am shaped like a lemon. People use my juice to make drinks. What am I?

_____

3. I hang on trees. There are many of me. In the autumn I fall to the ground. What am I?

_____

4. I may be sour, dill, or sweet. I come in several sizes. People eat me with sandwiches and hamburgers. What am I?

_____

5. I am a vegetable. I am full of leaves. People eat me in salads. What am I?

_____

6. I grow in your yard. I need rain and sunlight. In the summer I must be cut. What am I?

_____

Hidden Clovers

There are four four-leafed clovers in this field. Help the leprechaun find them. Color them green. Then draw and color four more gold coins in the leprechaun's pot.

I Know About St. Patrick's Day

Earth Day Fun

Earth Day Facts

- In 1960, Senator Gaylord Nelson began to make people aware of the need to take care of the earth. (A senator is someone who helps make laws.)

- It is everyone's responsibility to protect the earth. We have one earth—we must take care of it.

- The first Earth Day was celebrated on April 22, 1970.

- Today, people all over the world get involved in taking care of the earth.

- To protect the earth we must recycle, reuse, and reduce.

- We must keep the streams, rivers, and oceans pollution-free.

- Planting trees is another way to help the earth.

- Protecting rainforests is an important way to help protect the earth.

Earth Day Fun Activities

1. Organize a recycling drive at your school.

2. Help take care of the earth. Keep the playground clean.

3. Have a "beautification" day and plant flowers or a tree at school.

Earth Day

This is our earth.

We must take care of it! 2

Reduce. 3

Recycle. 4

Reuse. 5

Hand in hand, we can make a difference! 6

(Draw your idea.) How can you help the earth? 7

Doorknob Hanging Tree

Materials:

- one pattern (on following page) for each child
- colored pencils or crayons
- scissors

Directions for the following page:

1. Read the message written on the tree.
2. Carefully cut out the small circle in the tree.
3. Then, color and cut out the large tree pattern.
4. Take your "Doorknob Hanging Tree" home and place it on the door you use the most!

Doorknob Hanging Tree *(cont.)*

Cut Out Circle

Thank you for remembering to conserve energy and to recycle. Every little bit helps to preserve wildlife!

I Know About Earth Day

Easter Fun

Easter Facts

- Easter is celebrated in the Spring on a Sunday.

- Easter is a religious holiday for most Christians. It is a time to celebrate the Resurrection of Christ.

- Some people view Easter as a time to think about new life—baby animals, blooming plants, etc.

- Eggs are part of the Easter tradition. Eggs are colored, decorated, and hidden. Eggs represent new life.

- Many people enjoy an Easter dinner with family and friends.

- Easter lilies are also a symbol of new life. People decorate their homes and churches with these large, white lilies at Easter.

Easter Fun Activities

1. Sort and graph jellybeans.

2. Estimate the number of jellybeans in a jar.

3. Group jellybeans in sets of ten and count.

4. Dye and decorate hard-boiled eggs.

5. Have an egg hunt. Graph the number of eggs found by color.

6. Learn about rabbits.

7. Make a list of all the animals that are hatched from eggs.

Easter

The Easter Bunny is coming.

He is hopping down the street. 2

He is giving Easter eggs 3 to the boys and girls he meets. 4

Have your Easter basket ready . . . 5

he is hopping YOUR way . 6

To fill your Easter basket on this special day! 7

Origami Bunny

Bunnies are the most common symbol of Easter. To make origami bunnies you will need a 6" (15 cm) square of paper to fold. Follow the directions below to create a bunny while practicing origami, the Japanese art of paper folding.

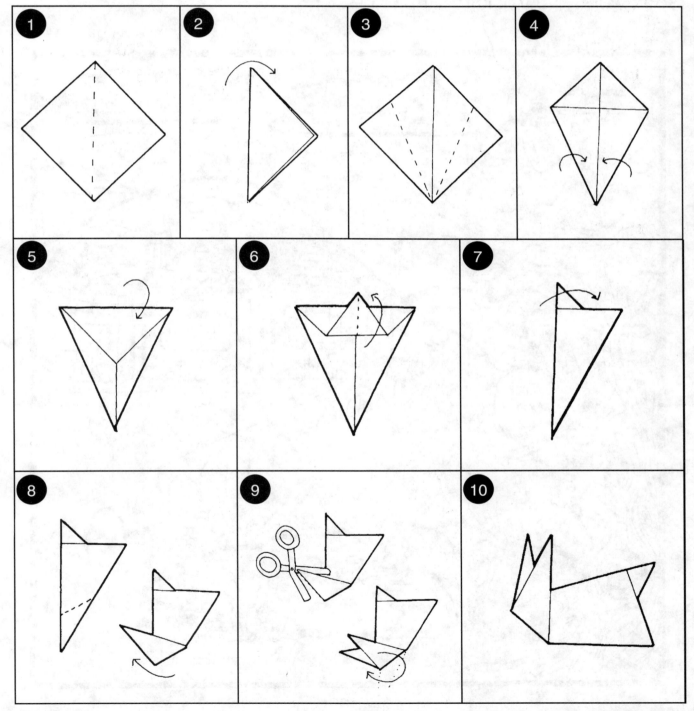

Help the Easter Bunny

Can this rabbit play a trick on you? He usually hides eggs, but today he hid these items: a hat, a baseball, a shirt, an umbrella, an ice cream cone, a heart, the number 5, a hot dog, a pencil, and a lollipop. Can you circle them?

Good work! Now color your picture.

46

Cotton Ball Chick

Materials

- Chick Body Pattern (on next page)
- Feet and Beak Patterns
- Construction Paper
- Scissors
- Glue
- Cotton Balls

Directions

1. Reproduce body pattern on white or yellow construction paper.
2. Reproduce feet and beak patterns on orange construction paper.
3. Cut out parts and glue together as shown in diagram.
4. Glue pieces of cotton to body of chick.

Feet

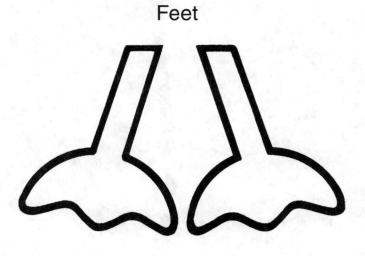

Beak

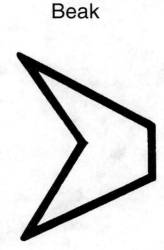

Cotton Ball Chick *(cont.)*

Body

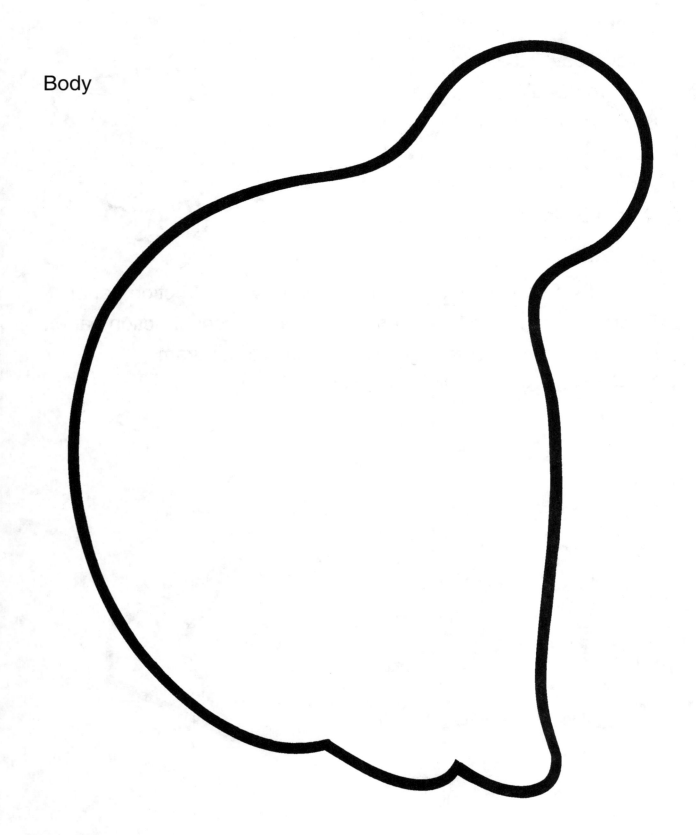

I Know About Easter

_____

_____

_____

_____

_____

_____

_____

Cinco de Mayo Fun

Cinco de Mayo Facts

- Cinco de Mayo means "the fifth of May" in Spanish.
- Cinco de Mayo is a Mexican holiday celebrating freedom and liberty.
- Mexican people remember the men who fought the French for freedom at Puebla, Mexico.
- Cinco de Mayo is celebrated with a fiesta. A fiesta is a party. The celebration used to take place in the center of town.
- Music is played, songs are sung, and dancers dance during Cinco de Mayo celebration.
- Sometimes, people celebrate with piñatas. Piñatas are very colorful and can be filled with many different things.

Cinco de Mayo Fun Activities

1. Locate Mexico on the globe. Discuss its location.
2. Chart a travel route on a map to Mexico.
3. Compare a sombrero to other types of hats.

4. Have a Mexican food tasting party. Try quesadillas, salsa and chips, guacamole, beans, corn tortillas, etc.
5. Listen to Mexican music and try a Mexican hat dance.
6. Make or buy a piñata and fill it with treats. Hang it up and take turns trying to break it, using a stick or plastic bat.

50

Cinco de Mayo

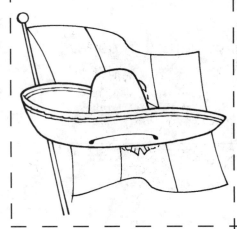

5

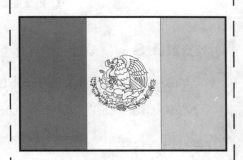

Cinco de Mayo means "the 5th of May."

Cinco de Mayo is a Mexican holiday.

2

The Mexican people remember the men who fought for freedom.

3

Cinco de Mayo is celebrated with a fiesta.

4

People sing and dance.

5

They also play music.

6

Often, children break piñatas filled with treats.

7

Cinco de Mayo

Mexican Place Mat

Materials

- One piece of construction paper
- Scissors
- Ruler
- 16 strips of construction paper
- Glue
- Pencil

Directions

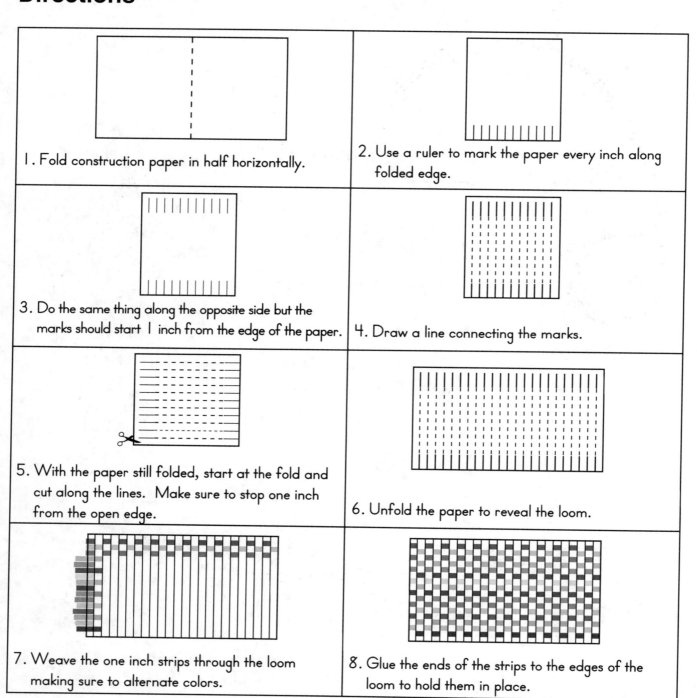

1. Fold construction paper in half horizontally.

2. Use a ruler to mark the paper every inch along folded edge.

3. Do the same thing along the opposite side but the marks should start 1 inch from the edge of the paper.

4. Draw a line connecting the marks.

5. With the paper still folded, start at the fold and cut along the lines. Make sure to stop one inch from the open edge.

6. Unfold the paper to reveal the loom.

7. Weave the one inch strips through the loom making sure to alternate colors.

8. Glue the ends of the strips to the edges of the loom to hold them in place.

I Know About Cinco de Mayo

Mother's Day Fun

Mother's Day Facts

- Mother's Day is the second Sunday in May each year in the United States.

- President Woodrow Wilson declared Mother's Day a national holiday on May 9, 1914.

- Mother's Day is a day to show our love for our mothers (or other special women) in special ways. Gifts, cards, and flowers are some presents given to mothers.

- Mother's Day is celebrated on different dates around the world.

- Many families celebrate Mother's Day with a breakfast or a dinner for Mom.

Mother's Day Fun Activities

1. Make Mother's Day cards.

2. Compose an acrostic poem, using "Mother" or "Mom" or "Grandma."

3. Invite mothers to lunch.

4. Invite a mom to read a story to the class.

5. Write about what you love most about your mom.

6. Surprise mom or a special caregiver by doing something special for her. Maybe finish a chore without being asked.

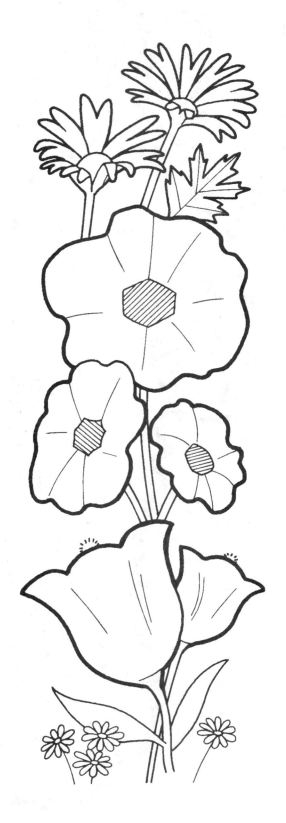

Mother's Day

I love my mom.

She takes care of me.

2

She washes my clothes and she reads to me.

3

How can I show her that I love her?

4

I've thought of a hundred things . . .

5

YES! Wait . . . it just hit me! I know just what to do . . .

6

. . . lots of hugs and kisses and an I Love You!

7

Standing Picture Frame

Materials

- Construction Paper
- Glue
- Scissors
- Crayons

Directions

1. Reproduce frame pieces on construction paper in spring colors.
2. Color design on frame front.
3. Cut out all pieces.
4. Fold frame front in half. Cut along solid lines to cut out center rectangle. Unfold frame front.
5. Glue front frame to back frame along two sides and bottom as shown below.
6. To make the stand, fold F flap to the right and E flap to the left. Glue C and D together.
7. To make the frame stand up, glue E and F to frame back, making the bottom edge even with bottom edge of frame.
8. Picture can be slipped between front and back frame from the top so it shows through rectangle.

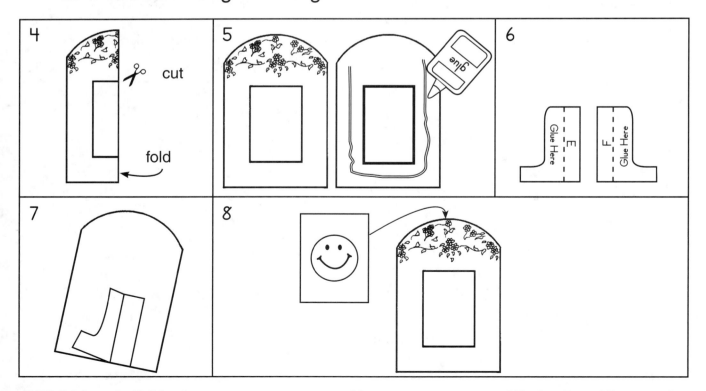

Standing Picture Frame *(cont.)*

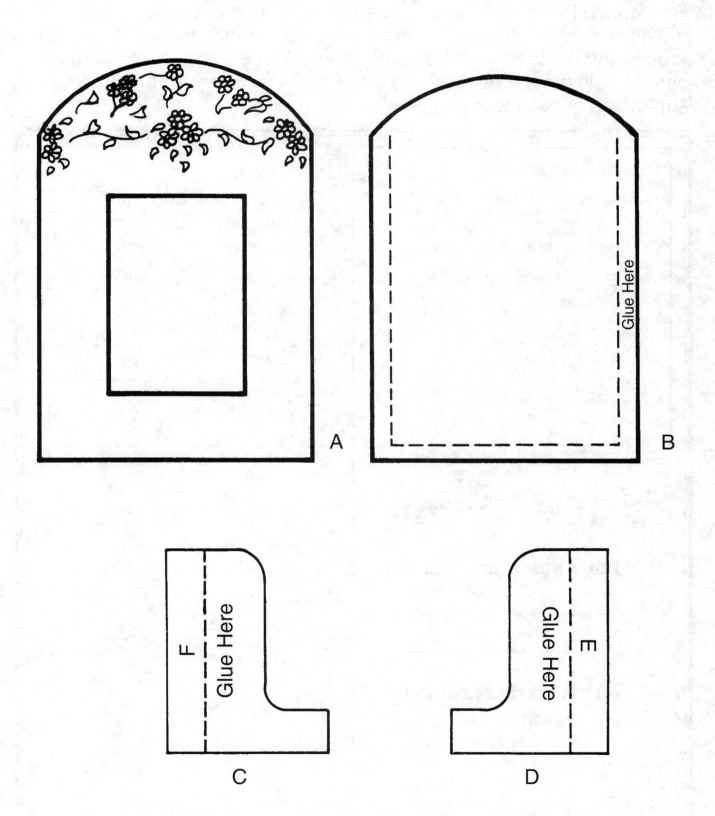

Mother's Day Card

Reproduce this page to create the inside of a card. Draw a picture of mother inside the frame. Complete the statements about mother. Cut around the outer box. Write a very special letter to Mom. Fold the card in half. On the front draw a picture of you and your mom doing something special together.

Dear Mom,

_____

_____

_____

_____

_____

_____

_____

_____

_____

_____

_____

_____

Super Mom

I love you because . . .

_____

_____

You are the best mother because . . .

_____

_____

Love,

_____

"Feel Good" Jar

Materials

- Small Canning Jar with Dome Lid and Band
- 7" (18 cm) Square of Fabric
- Construction Paper (various colors)
- Pen
- Pinking Shears
- Scissors

Directions

1. Cut the construction paper into 1" x 12" (2.5 cm x 30 cm) long strips. Give each child ten strips. On each strip have children write why their mother makes them feel good.
   Sentence starters can include:

   You make me feel good when . . .

   I like it when...

   My favorite thing that we do together is . . .

   After writing the strips, have students accordion fold or roll the strips. Have them place them in the jar.

2. Using the pinking shears, cut the sides of the fabric.

3. 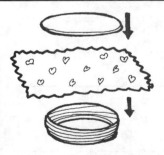 Separate the dome lid and band. Place the dome lid down on a table. Have students place the fabric square evenly over it. Gently have them snap the dome lid and the fabric into the band. Place the fabric-covered dome lid and band onto the jar and twist shut.

4. Have them take the jar home to Mother. You may wish to include directions for the jar to let Mother take a strip out whenever she wants to "feel good."

I Know About Mother's Day

Memorial Day Fun

Memorial Day Facts

- Memorial Day is a patriotic holiday in the United States. It is celebrated on the last Monday in May each year.

- It began as a day to honor the men and women who died in the Civil War.

- On Memorial Day we honor all the men and women who have died in all the wars fought by the United States.

- Memorial Day is celebrated in many ways. Many businesses, schools, and banks close in honor of the holiday.

- Often, families go to the cemetery to add flags to the grave sites of war veterans.

- Parades and picnics are other ways this holiday is celebrated.

Memorial Day Fun Activities

1. Discuss the meaning of the word "memorial."

2. Make flags to decorate the classroom or homes.

3. Invite a guest speaker from the military to visit the class.

4. Make cards for the veterans in the community.

5. Compose an acrostic poem with the word "memorial."

Memorial Day

Memorial Day is a patriotic holiday.

It began as a day to honor men and women who died in the Civil War. 2

Today we honor all who have fought for our freedom. 3

Memorial Day is celebrated on the last Monday in May. 4

Many businesses close in honor of Memorial Day. 5

STORE

Closed

Some people hang the American flag outside their home. 6

I am thankful for my freedom! 7

Honoring Our Flag

The flag of the United States is a symbol to be treated with respect. Here are some rules for displaying the flag with honor. Cut out each of these boxes that hold the rules. Paste or glue them under the appropriate pictures.

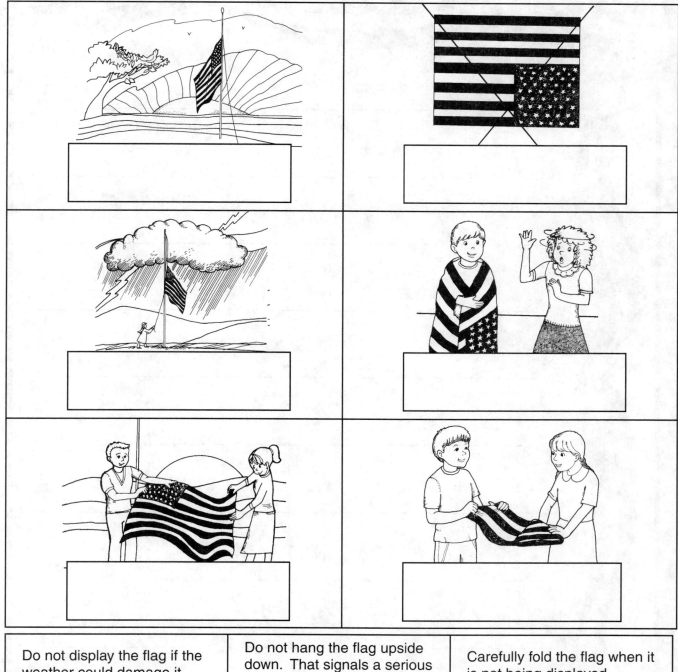

Do not display the flag if the weather could damage it.	Do not hang the flag upside down. That signals a serious emergency.	Carefully fold the flag when it is not being displayed.
Do not let the flag touch the ground.	The flag of the United States may not be used for clothing. Use the colors, not the flag.	Display the flag from sunrise to sunset.

I Know About Memorial Day

Father's Day Fun

Father's Day Facts

- In 1966, President Lyndon B. Johnson declared Father's Day a national holiday.

- Father's Day is celebrated the third Sunday in June.

- We celebrate Father's Day to show love for our fathers or other men who are special to us.

- We honor fathers on this day with special gifts and cards.

- Some families have a special breakfast or dinner for Dad on this day.

Father's Day Fun Activities

1. Make Father's Day Cards.

2. Compose an acrostic poem, using the word "Father" or "Dad" or "Grandpa."

3. Invite fathers to lunch.

4. Invite a father to read a story to the class.

5. Write about what you love most about your dad.

Father's Day

I love my dad.

He does so much for me.   1

He helps me ride my bike.   2

He helps me climb a tree.   3

I want to make him feel special . . . and I know just what to do.   4

I'll hug his neck . . .   5

. . . I'll hold his hand—   6

I'll say...

I LOVE YOU   7

Pencil Holder

Materials

- Construction Paper
- Crayons
- Scissors
- Glue

- One Soup Can—Cleaned with Label Removed

Directions

1. Reproduce pattern pieces on white construction paper. Color and cut out all pieces.
2. Glue the "dad" rectangle on soup can.
3. Glue the arms to sides of the can. Fold them slightly forward for a better 3-D effect.
4. Glue legs to bottom of can. Legs can be bent to "sit" on edge of table or left flat.

Pencil Holder *(cont.)*

Duck Change Holder

Make this container for Dad to hold his change.

Materials

- 1/2 lb. (.22 kg) Small Butter Tub
- White Construction Paper
- Crayons
- Scissors
- Glue
- Patterns (next page)

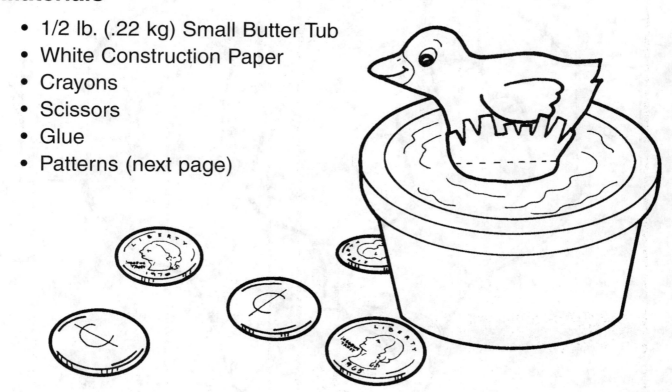

Directions

1. Reproduce the pattern pieces on white construction paper. Color and cut out.
2. Glue water circle to the clear plastic butter tub cover.
3. Fold duck along broken lines and at the space between heads.
4. Glue duck together except tabs.
5. Glue tab A to C on water.
6. Glue tab B to D on water.
7. Curl grasses by wrapping or folding around a pencil.
8. Glue grasses to tabs A and B to cover them.
9. Put the cover on the tub.

Duck Change Holder *(cont.)*

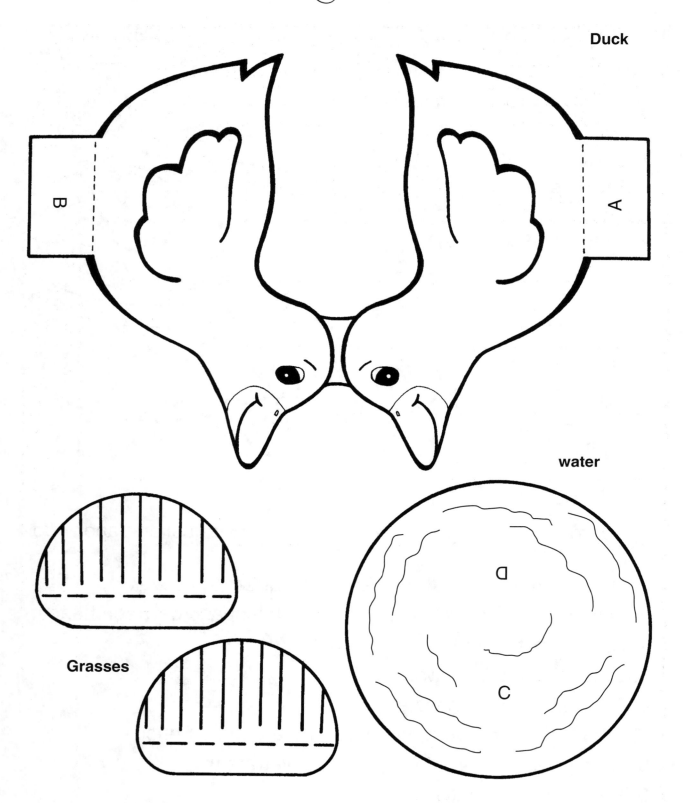

Duck

B

A

water

Grasses

D

C

I Know About Father's Day

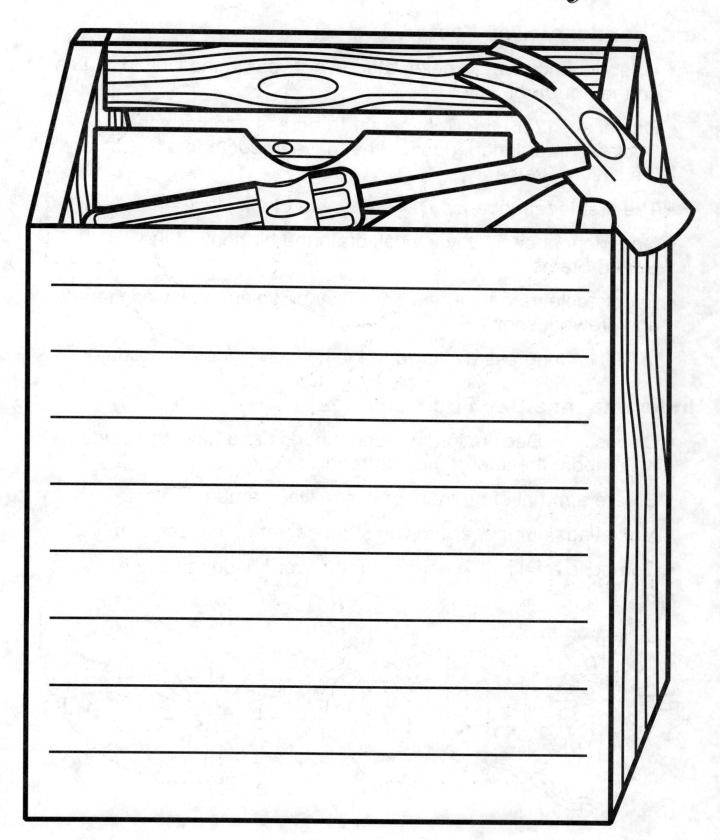

Independence Day Fun

Independence Day Facts

- Independence Day is celebrated every year in the United States on the Fourth of July.

- On July 4, 1776, the Continental Congress adopted the Declaration of Independence that gave freedom to all who lived in the United States.

- The first Independence Day celebration took place on July 4, 1777.

- On Independence Day we celebrate the birthday of the United States.

- People celebrate Independence Day by going to picnics, parades, and firework shows.

- In 1941, Congress declared the 4th of July a federal holiday.

Independence Day Fun Activities

- Discuss the Declaration of Independence and have the students write about the importance of freedom.

- Create a mural of an Independence Day parade.

- Make flags and paper fireworks to decorate the classroom.

- Compose an acrostic poem with the word "independence."

Independence Day

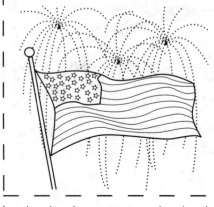

Independence Day is a patriotic holiday.

It began in the United States as a day to celebrate freedom.

2

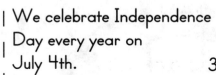

We celebrate Independence Day every year on July 4th.

3

Some people celebrate by having a picnic at the park.

4

Others celebrate by attending a parade.

5

Most people watch a fireworks show at night.

6

Independence Day is a loud, joyous holiday.

7

4th of July Bike

Directions: Pretend that you are going to ride this bike in a 4th of July parade. Design and color it the way you would like it to look.

74

I Know About Independence Day

_____

_____

_____

_____

_____

_____

_____

_____

_____

_____

_____

Labor Day Fun

Labor Day Facts

- President Grover Cleveland declared Labor Day a national holiday in 1894.

- Labor Day is celebrated on the first Monday in September in the United States.

- Labor Day is the day we celebrate "workers."

- Some workers provide services—teachers, bankers, policemen.

- Some workers produce goods—bakers, factory workers, farmers.

- Labor Day is celebrated in different ways. Many people picnic and barbecue and enjoy outdoor recreational activities.

Labor Day Fun Activities

1. Invite workers and/or parents from the community to come and talk about their jobs.

2. Have the students write about what they want to be when they grow up. Then, graph the different careers chosen.

3. Play the game of charades and act out the tasks different workers perform.

4. Make a list of tools that are used by different professions.

Labor Day

Everyone has a job to do.

Some people produce goods . . .
bakers, factory workers,
farmers.

2

Some people provide
services . . .
teachers, bankers, policemen.

3

Everyone works together
in a community.

4

Labor Day is the day
we celebrate "workers."

5

You have a job too . . .

6

Your job is to do your best
in school.

7

"You've Got a Raise"

A Labor Day Card Game

Players: Two or three

Directions:

1. For each set of cards, reproduce 3 copies of the career card page that follows.

2. Cut out all cards. Throw away two copies of the card that reads "You've Got a Raise!" There will be 33 cards to a set.

3. Mix the cards, face down. Deal 5 to each player. Put the remaining cards in a pile face down.

4. If a player is dealt four identical cards, he or she makes a "book" of these and places them face up in front of him or her.

5. After the players have eliminated their "books" from their playing hands, the first player selects an unseen card from the pile. Then the player checks to see if he or she can make a "book" with this additional card.

6. The second player then takes a turn.

7. The player who ends up with the "You've Got a Raise!" card wins.

Variations:

- Two identical cards can also make a "book." This enables the game to be played at a quicker pace.

- This game can also be played like "Go Fish" or "Old Maid."

"You've Got a Raise" *(cont.)*

Career Cards

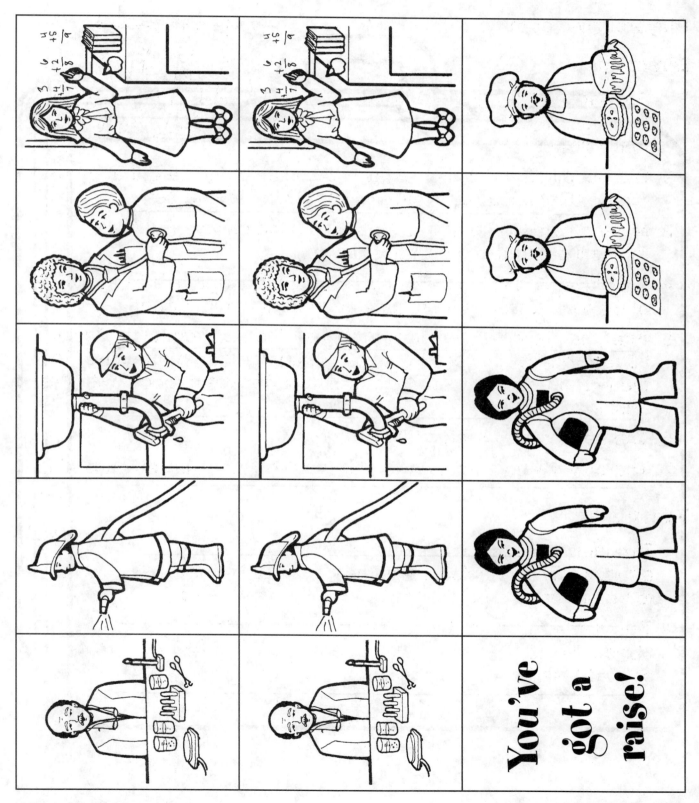

I Know About Labor Day

Columbus Day Fun

Columbus Day Facts

- We celebrate Columbus Day to honor Columbus' voyage to the New World.

- Columbus Day is celebrated on the second Monday in October.

- Christopher Columbus set sail from Spain in search of the New World on August 3, 1492.

- He was in search of an easier route to Asia for spice merchants.

- Queen Isabella of Spain paid for Columbus' voyages.

- Columbus had three ships. The ships were named the Niña, the Pinta, and the Santa Maria.

- Columbus Day is celebrated with parades.

Columbus Day Fun Activities

1. Chart Christopher Columbus' voyage from Spain to the New World on a map or a globe.

2. Turn three large boxes into the three ships. Take turns acting out the voyage.

3. Discuss what it might be like to be confined to a ship for 37 days. What would be enjoyable? What would be difficult?

4. Discuss the value of spices in foods and household items. Have students bring in different spices and compare them.

Christopher
Columbus

Christopher Columbus
was a sailor.

He wanted to find a shorter
way to Asia. Columbus
hoped to find gold
and riches.   2

He asked the king and queen
of Spain for money and ships.
3

He sailed with three ships:
the Niña, the Pinta, and the
Santa Maria.   4

Columbus set sail from Spain
in 1492.
5

The voyage lasted for
37 days.   6

He made several trips to the
New World.
7

Supplies for Columbus

Columbus sailed on a ship across the Atlantic Ocean. What supplies did he need for his voyage? In the space under the ship draw and label the supplies Columbus needed for his journey. Color the ship.

I Know About Columbus Day

Halloween Fun

Halloween Facts

- Halloween is celebrated on October 31st.
- In some cultures, Halloween is a time to celebrate the end of the harvest season.
- During Halloween, some children dress up in costumes and go trick-or-treating. Others have parties, try apple-bobbing, or go on hayrides.
- Follow these safety tips when you are trick-or-treating:
    1. Always trick-or-treat in a group or with an adult.
    2. Trick-or-treat at houses that are well lit.
    3. Always look both ways before crossing the street.
    4. Wear reflective and flame-retardant clothing.
    5. Carry a flashlight.
    6. Have an adult check all treats before eating them.

Halloween Fun Activities

1. Measure objects, using non-standard units of measure such as candy corn, mini erasers, or mini boxes of raisins.
2. Put various individually wrapped candies in a jar: estimate, sort, and graph the contents.
3. Graph students' favorite candies.
4. Measure the circumference of a pumpkin.
5. Carve a jack-o-lantern.
6. Count the number of seeds found in a pumpkin.
7. Bake and eat pumpkin seeds.
8. Bake or purchase a pumpkin pie for snack.

Halloween

Black cats, witches . . .

and flying bats. 2

Scarecrow, hay bales . . . 3

pumpkins and hats. 4

Apple bobbin', hayrides . . . 5

and lots of things to eat. 6

October 31 is time to

Trick-or-Treat. 7

Drawing Halloween Characters *(cont.)*

Directions: Draw a cat. Follow the steps in each box.

1. Draw half an oval. 	4. Complete your cat with whiskers and hair to make your cat look scary. 
2. Draw another half oval inside the first oval. 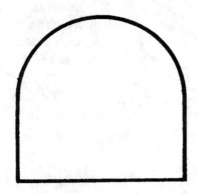	Draw your Halloween cat here.
3. Draw half-circle for a head. Add eyebrows, eyes, nose, mouth, and ear shapes as shown. 	

Halloween Riddles

My hat is black.
My face is green.
My laugh is mean.
I ride a broom
On Halloween.
What am I?

I like to stay
Just out of sight.
If you see me,
I might be white.
I float through houses
In the black of night.
What am I?

I grew on a vine,
Right on the ground.
I have a big smile,
All orange and round.
What am I?

I fly at night.
I hunt by sound.
I live in a cave
And sleep upside down.
People are scared;
They shouldn't be.
I eat mice and bugs.
Please don't hurt me.
What am I?

My door is gone.
My windows cracked.
Ghosts float through walls
And then float back.
You hear strange noises,
Bam, bang, and whack.
What am I?

My eyes are gold.
My fur is black.
I hiss and spit
And arch my back.
My claws are sharp.
I might attack.
What am I?

88

Make Your Own Faces!

Draw a different face on each pumpkin. Write a title or name for each one.

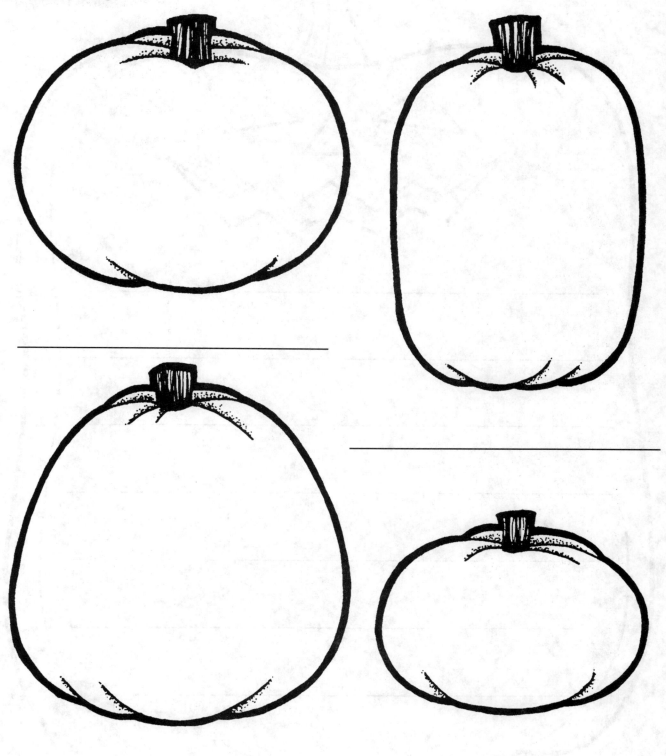

I Know About Halloween

Thanksgiving Fun

Thanksgiving Facts

- The Pilgrims sailed to the New World on a ship called the Mayflower.
- The Mayflower was 113 feet long.
- The Pilgrims set sail from Plymouth, England, on September 6, 1620.
- There were 102 Pilgrims on the Mayflower.
- The journey to the New World took 65 days.
- An agreement called the Mayflower Compact was written to set rules for life in the new land.
- The first home the Pilgrims built was called the common house.
- All the Pilgrims lived together in the common house until individual homes were built.
- Only 51 of the Pilgrims survived to celebrate the first Thanksgiving feast.
- In 1863, Abraham Lincoln made Thanksgiving Day a national holiday.

Thanksgiving Fun Activities

1. Have a class Thanksgiving feast.
2. Make a paper chain to represent the length of the Mayflower (113 feet).
3. Take 113 steps (nonstandard measurement) and compare to 113 feet (standard measurement).
4. Use a calendar to identify the number of months and weeks it took the Pilgrims to get to the New World (65 days).
5. Use counters to identify the number of pilgrims—102. Group into sets of 5 or 10.

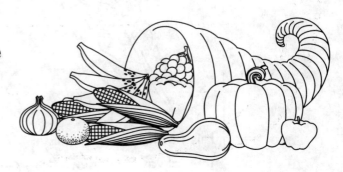

Mr. Turkey

Mr. Turkey gobbles and waddles all around. . .

on a farm . . .   2

or in the forest is where he can be found.   3

He has a great big wattle.   4

and lots of feathers, too!   5

His feathers are so shiny they always look new.   6

Gobble, Waddle, Gobble — You know what to do!   7

Giving Thanks Turkey

Materials

- Crayons
- Scissors
- Pencil
- Glue

Directions

1. Give one copy of page 94 to each student.
2. Have students brainstorm things that they are thankful for.
3. Have students pick nine things to write in feathers. Have them write one thing per feather.
4. Color the feathers and the turkey parts.
5. Cut out the pieces.
6. Glue the tail pieces behind the body.

I Am Thankful For

I am thankful for

I am thankful for

I am thankful for

I am thankful for

I am thankful for

I am thankful for

I Know About Thanksgiving Day

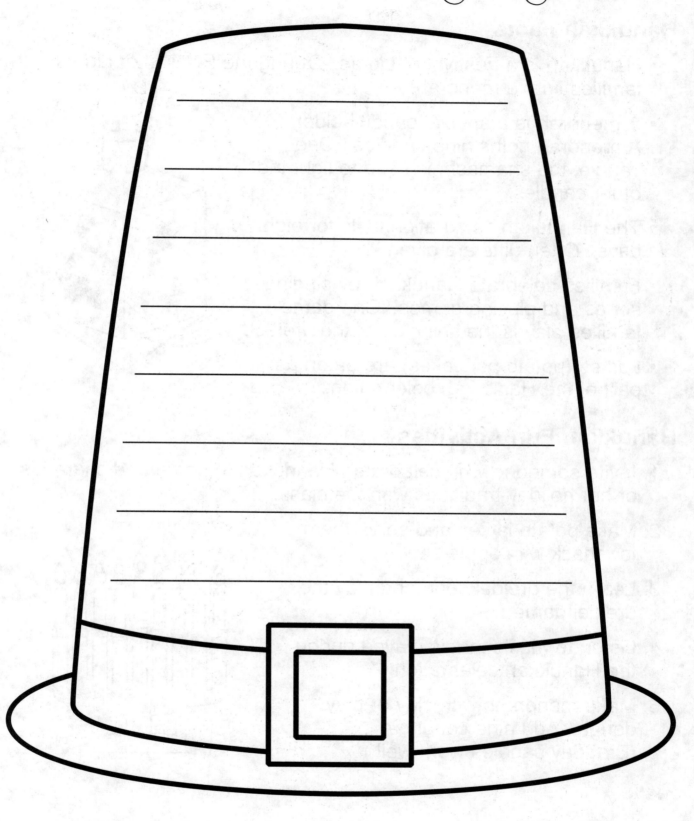

Hanukkah Fun

Hanukkah Facts

- Hanukkah is a Festival of Lights. During the Festival of Lights families light a menorah.

- A menorah is a special candleholder. A menorah holds nine candles. One candle, the shamash, is used to light the other candles.

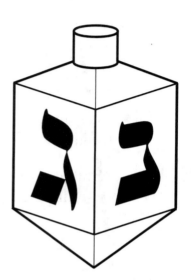

- The Hannukah celebration lasts for eight days. Often gifts are given.

- Families celebrate Hanukkah by singing songs and playing games. One game families play is the spinning of the dreidel.

- Latkes (potato pancakes) are eaten as part of the Hanukkah celebration.

Hanukkah Fun Activities

1. Invite someone who celebrates Hannukah to come and share his or her holiday traditions with the class.

2. Make potato latkes and serve them for snack with apple sauce.

3. Learn the dreidel song and play the dreidel game.

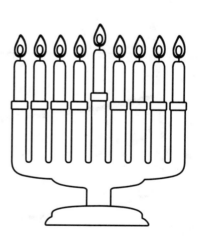

4. Listen to music that is played during the Hanukkah celebration.

5. Make menorahs with clay or play dough. Add nine candles. (Birthday candles work well.)

Hanukkah

Hanukkah is celebrated by the Jewish people. 1

It is a Festival of Lights. 2

The celebration lasts eight days. 3

The celebration begins by lighting the menorah. 4

A menorah has nine candles. The shamash candle is used to light the other eight candles. 5

Often gifts are given. 6

Families sing songs and play games. 7

Hanging Dreidel

Materials

- Index Paper
- Scissors
- Markers
- Tape
- Glue
- String
- Glitter

Directions

Reproduce both pieces of the dreidel onto index paper. Decorate. Slit the pieces on the dashed lines and slip the pieces together as shown. Tape them in the creases. Punch a hole in the top. Thread a piece of yarn or string and hang as a decoration.

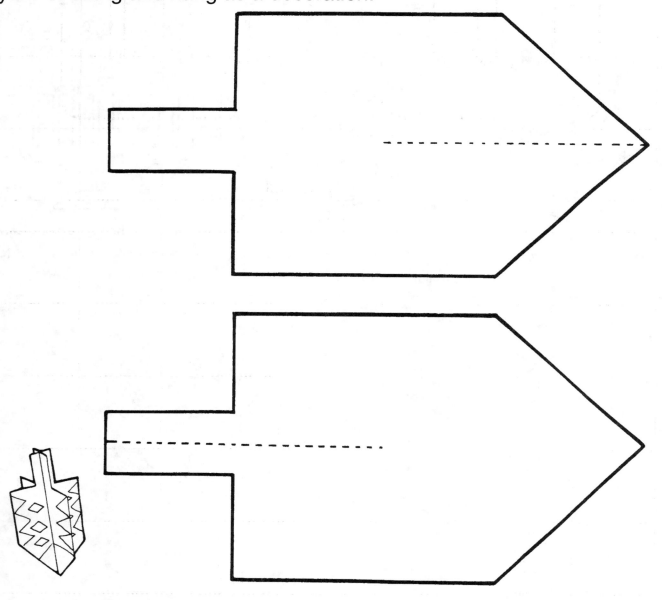

You Can Draw It!

Copy the picture one square at a time onto the bottom grid. Color your picture when you have finished your drawing.

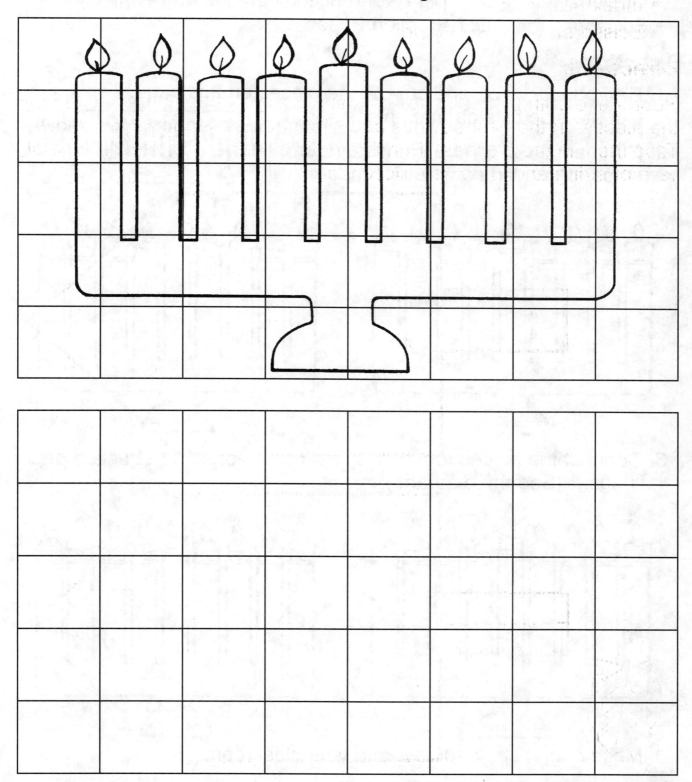

Hanukkah Garland

Materials

- Crayons
- Scissors
- Multiple Reproductions of This Page
- Construction Paper
- Tape

Directions

1. Reproduce, color, and cut out the pieces on this page. Cut the side slits on each piece.

2. Cut many ¾" x 5" (1.9 cm x 12.70 cm) strips of colored construction paper.

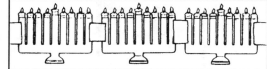

3. Connect the pieces together by making colored construction paper "rings." (See the diagram.)

4. Make a long chain to decorate your classroom.

I Know About Hanukkah

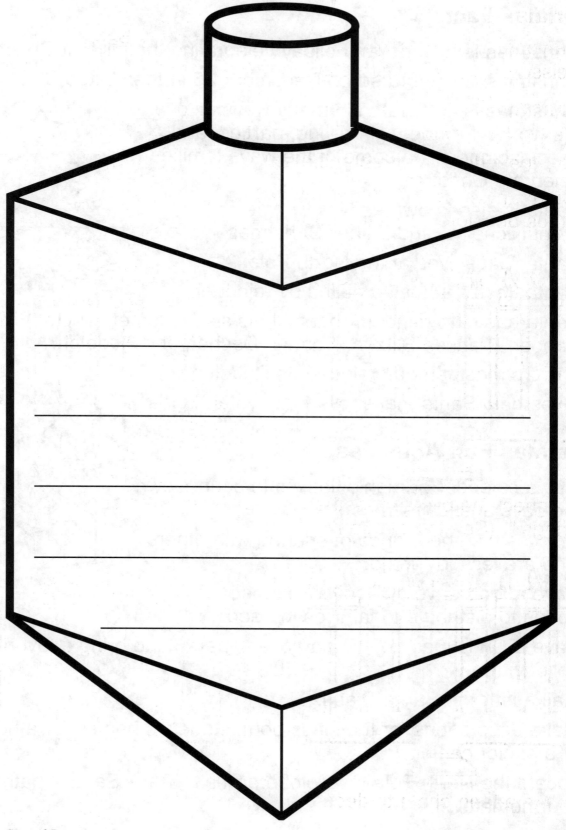

Christmas Fun

Christmas Facts

- Christmas is a Christian holiday celebrating the birth of Christ.
- Christmas is celebrated on December 25 in the United States.
- Christmas is celebrated in many ways all over the world. Parades, gift giving, parties, and special dinners are some of the ways families celebrate Christmas.
- Santa is also known as Kris Kringle, Saint Nicholas, and Father Christmas.
- Santa Claus lives at the North Pole.
- Santa travels in a sled pulled by reindeer.
- Santa has nine reindeer that pull his sled: Comet, Cupid, Vixen, Dancer, Prancer, Blitzen, Donner, Dasher, and Rudolph.
- Santa's most famous reindeer is Rudolph.
- Elves help Santa make toys for boys and girls.

Christmas Fun Activities

1. Use a calendar or manipulatives to count down the days until Christmas.
2. Discuss the importance of sharing with others who are less fortunate.
3. Have a food drive and collect canned goods to distribute to families in need.

4. Have a Christmas goodie party. Ask parents to bring a favorite holiday treat.
5. Mail a letter to Santa Claus.
6. Make decorations for the classroom, student's homes, or a hospital or a senior center.
7. Locate the North Pole on a globe or map. Track Santa's path to your hometown.

102

What Do You See At Christmas?

What do you see at Christmas?

Christmas trees 1

What do you see at Christmas?

ornaments 2

What do you see at Christmas?

angels 3

What do you see at Christmas?

candy canes 4

What do you see at Christmas?

presents 5

What do you see at Christmas?

reindeer 6

What do you see at Christmas?

Santa Claus 7

Christmas Bookmarks

Materials

- bookmark pattern
- crayons or colored markers
- tagboard
- scissors

Directions

1. Trace around pattern onto tagboard.
2. Draw a Christmas object, animal, or other shapes at the top of the bookmark pattern or use the thee pattern on this page.
3. Cut out the book mark pattern.
4. Color the design with crayons or marking pens.

Holiday Scene

Color the numbers the correct color and a holiday scene will appear.

1- red   2- orange   3- yellow   4- blue   5- green   6-brown

I Know About Christmas

Kwanzaa Fun

Kwanzaa Facts

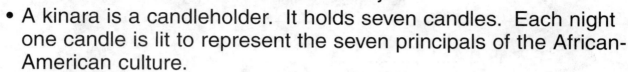

- Kwanzaa is an African-American celebration created to celebrate family, community, and culture.
- The holiday begins on December 26th and lasts for seven days.
- Symbols for Kwanzaa include the kinara, the mkeka, and the kikombe cha umoja.
- A kinara is a candleholder. It holds seven candles. Each night one candle is lit to represent the seven principals of the African-American culture.
- The seven principles are—unity, self-determination, collective work and responsibility, cooperative economics, purpose, creativity, and faith.
- A mkeka is a special, colorful placemat used to display fruits and vegetables. It represents traditon and history.
- The kikombe cha umoja is a large cup or goblet that stands for staying together.
- On the seventh day of Kwanzaa, many families gather for a dinner called Karamu.
- Dancing, singing, feasting, and gift-giving are some of the ways Kwanzaa is celebrated.

Kwanzaa Fun Activities

1. Invite a celebrant of Kwanzaa from the community to talk about the holiday.
2. Have a fruit tasting party.
3. Graph the classes' favorite fruits.
4. Have children weave a "mkeka," using construction-paper strips.
5. Create kinaras, using clay and birthday candles. Decorate them with sequins, beads, tiles, and/or jewels.

Kwanzaa

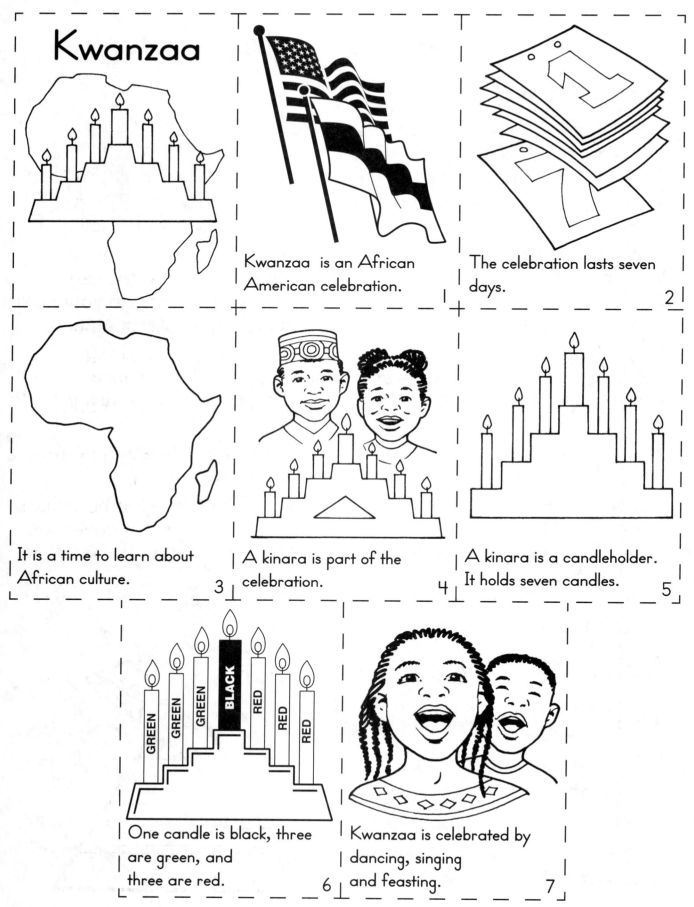

Kwanzaa is an African American celebration.

The celebration lasts seven days.

2

It is a time to learn about African culture.

3

A kinara is part of the celebration.

4

A kinara is a candleholder. It holds seven candles.

5

GREEN GREEN GREEN BLACK RED RED RED

One candle is black, three are green, and three are red.

6

Kwanzaa is celebrated by dancing, singing and feasting.

7

Kwanzaa Gift

Materials

- Copy of bookmark and Tag
- Construction Paper
- Crayons   • Yarn   • Hole Punch
- Scissors   • Stapler/Glue/Tape

Directions

1. Decorate the bookmark and tag patterns. Be sure to include your own special message on the bookmark.
2. Cut out the bookmark and tag.
3. Punch a hole inside the circle.
4. Thread a piece of yarn or ribbon through the hole.
5. Glue, tape, or staple the tag to the end of the yarn or ribbon.

Suggestion: To make the bookmark more durable, laminate or cover with clear adhesive paper.

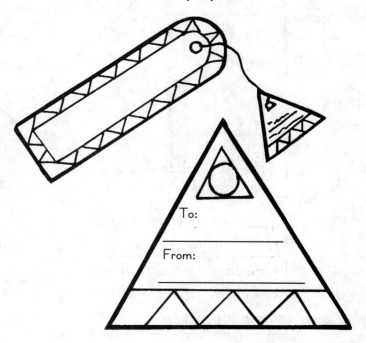

To: _____

From: _____

Kinara and Candle Pattern

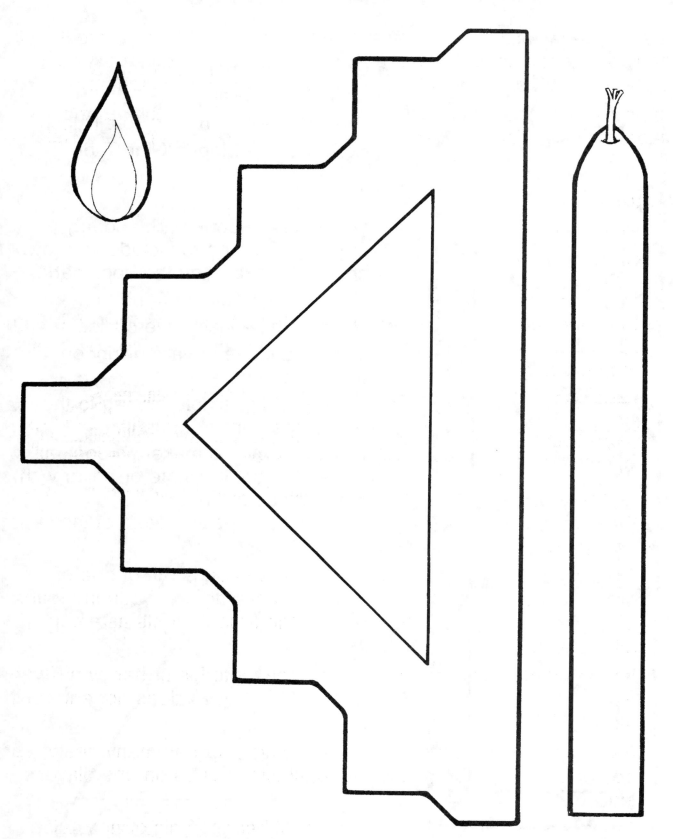

Mankalah

The Arabs call this game Kalah. They brought it to Africa where it has many different names. In East Africa, it is called Mankala. In West Africa, it is called Owara. In South Africa, it is known as Ohora.

You can make this game out of an empty egg carton. Look at the diagram below. The end sections are the Kalahs. Each player's Kalah is on his or her right. These sections count as cups during the game.

Materials

- Empty Egg Carton
- Dried Beans
- Scissors
- Tape or GAlue

Directions

1. Build the game board by separating the top and bottom of the egg carton. Cut the top section in half and affix each half to a side of the bottom section, as shown in the illustration.

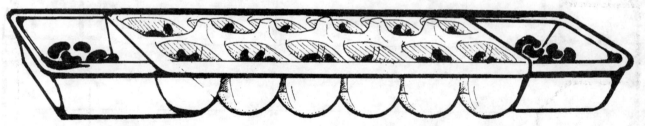

2. Play starts when the players put three beans into each of the cups on their own sides.

3. The first player begins by taking all of the beans out of one of his or her cups, and moving to the right, dropping one bean into each of the next three cups. (Remember, the Kalah counts as a cup after play begins.)

4. If the first player is able to drop the bean into his or her own Kalah, he/she gets another turn. If the last (third) bean does not end up in his/her own Kalah, it becomes the other player's turn.

5. Each player continue to take turns trying to get as many beans as possible into his/her own Kalah, until all the cups on one player's side are empty.

6. The winner is the player with the most beans in his or her Kalah.

I Know About Kwanzaa